NFTs Unraveled

Digital Art, Collectibles, and the Blockchain

Table of Contents

Chapter 1. Introduction

In the ever-evolving landscape of technology, a vibrant phenomenon has captured imaginations and launched uncountable digital ventures; they're known as Non-Fungible Tokens (NFTs). Our Special Report, "NFTs Unraveled: Digital Art, Collectibles, and the Blockchain," distills this complex yet fascinating subject into easily digestible pieces. We delve into the heart of digital art and collectibles, unraveling the mystery of the blockchain technology that underpins them. This report is not just for tech enthusiasts and art aficionados, but for anyone curious to navigate the frontiers of the digital era. With an engaging mix of in-depth analysis, accessible language, and illuminating real-world examples, this report promises a journey through the dynamic universe of NFTs, bringing you up to speed on one of the most intriguing innovations of our time. Let's demystify the complexity together!

Chapter 2. Unveiling Non-Fungible Tokens: An Introduction

The transformative wave of digitalization hasn't stopped its inertia at financial systems or e-commerce but has elegantly infiltrated the realm of art, collectibles, and unique digital assets — the very concept we name as 'Non-Fungible Tokens, or NFTs'. A unique product of the creative marriage between digital art and the disruptive blockchain technology, NFTs have quickly risen to prominence in the internet-savvy world, intriguing veterans and novel enthusiasts alike.

2.1. A Primer on Fungibility

To truly grasp the concept of Non-Fungible Tokens, it would be best to start by understanding what 'fungibility' means. Simply put, fungibility represents the property of a good or a commodity whose individual 'units' are interchangeable with one another. For instance, consider the currency we use daily — it doesn't matter whether you have a particular one-dollar bill or another, as all one-dollar bills share the same value.

Consequently, non-fungibility implies uniqueness. A non-fungible item cannot be substituted by any other; it's unique in its rights. A painting by Picasso, for example, is non-fungible. If you were to exchange it for a different painting, even by the same artist, you would end up with a fundamentally different item.

2.2. Non-Fungible Tokens & Their Characteristics

Derived from this concept, the term 'Non-Fungible Token' alludes to a type of digital asset, where each token is unique and cannot be substituted by any other. This contrasts with cryptocurrencies, like Bitcoin or Ethereum, which are fungible by nature. The tokens are stored on a blockchain, a type of decentralized digital ledger, which ensures the ownership and represent an immutable record of provenance.

The uniqueness of NFTs comes with an array of desirable characteristics:

- Immutable Provenance: Since NFTs are built on the blockchain, they offer an unalterable record of ownership. This means that an NFT token can showcase its entire history, from creation to the present day, with all its previous owners listed.

- Indivisibility: Unlike cryptocurrencies, which can be traded in fractions, NFTs are indivisible. They are bought, sold or traded as a whole, primarily because dividing an NFT would inevitably lead to the loss of its intrinsic value

- Interoperability: NFTs also offer a considerable degree of interoperability, achieved through the implementation of specific standard protocols on Ethereum blockchain (like the ERC721 and ERC1155). This means that tokens created on one platform can often be sold or traded on another.

2.3. How Do NFTs Work?

NFTs operate on the principles of blockchain technology — the same underlying technology that powers cryptocurrencies. The Ethereum blockchain is currently the most popular for creating NFTs, due to its smart contract functionality. However, other blockchains are now also venturing into NFTs, including Binance Smart Chain and Flow.

To mint an NFT, certain information gets encoded onto a token on the blockchain. That information typically includes who owns the token and a link to the digital asset itself. This link can point to anything digitally unique: a digital artwork, a song, a tweet, or even virtual real estate.

Once an NFT is created, it can be bought, sold or traded on a multitude of online marketplaces. Every time an NFT changes hands, its transaction history gets updated on the blockchain. This functionality ensures the authenticity of NFTs and proves their scarcity.

2.4. The NFT Revolution in Digital Art

The NFT revolution has had an enormous impact on the digital art world. For the first time, artists can sell their digital art directly to a global audience without intermediaries such as galleries or auction houses. They also can script royalties into their work, ensuring they receive compensation every time their art is resold.

Furthermore, NFTs play a crucial role in establishing provenance in the digital world. Before NFTs, copying a digital artwork was as simple as right-clicking and saving the file. With NFTs and blockchain technology, the owner of a digital artwork can be indisputably verified.

2.5. Challenges & Criticisms

Despite the potential of NFTs, there are also several criticisms and challenges to consider. The first and foremost is the environmental impact of blockchain technology, which consumes a large amount of energy.

Secondly, there are concerns related to intellectual property and copyright infringement in the NFT space. Since anyone can mint an NFT, it is possible to mint an NFT of a digital asset one does not own.

Thirdly, extreme price volatility presents significant financial risk. Many NFTs have sold for astronomical prices, but their values can fluctuate wildly and rapidly.

As we advance further into the digital era, the evolution of NFTs is undoubtedly a space to watch. This novel technology has already started reshaping the boundaries of art, ownership, and uniqueness in the digital world. Regardless of the challenges, NFTs have unignorably forged a new frontier in the digital landscape that can no longer be overlooked.

Chapter 3. The Origins and Evolution of NFTs

To dive into the universe of NFTs, we first need to understand the circumstances that led to their birth. In their simplest form, NFTs are digital assets that represent ownership or proof of authenticity of a unique item or content in the digital realm, using blockchain technology. They cannot be replicated or substituted, meaning they are non-fungible. The concept may seem novel, but in reality, their roots stretch back to the earliest days of human economic activity.

3.1. The Pre-Blockchain Era

In ancient times, civilizations used unique items such as shells, gold, and precious stones to signify value. These were non-fungible in nature; each item's value was inherent and unique. As societies evolved, trading systems came into existence, where unique items began to lose their individual distinctiveness, replaced by standardization, which was essential for economies of scale. Currency was invented, which led to the creation of financial systems that form the basis of the modern economy.

By the end of the 20th century, the advent of the internet had changed the value system completely. We moved from the tangible to the intangible, the physical to the digital. Everything began to have a digital representation, from photographs to music, books, and identity. But there was a problem. In this digital world, anything could be replicated perfectly, creating a crisis of authenticity and value. The need for a solution to verify digital uniqueness and ownership gave rise to the concept of digital scarcity, the seed from which NFTs would eventually grow.

3.2. Advent of the Blockchain

The solution to the digital authenticity crisis lay in blockchain technology. Introduced with the creation of Bitcoin in 2009, blockchain allows for the creation of a decentralized, immutable ledger, a series of secure, verifiable transactions that exists across multiple networks. This feature enabled the solution to the double-spending problem in digital currency, where a digital asset can be spent more than once, as it could be copied exactly.

Nonetheless, Bitcoin was a fungible token; each unit of bitcoin was the same as any other, just like money. This fungibility was key to Bitcoin's function as a medium of exchange. However, the importance of blockchain technology was not just about creating digital currency. It was the ability to create unique, verifiable digital assets that held the most promise.

This promise began to be fulfilled with the creation of Ethereum in 2015. Ethereum expanded on the concepts introduced by Bitcoin and added a critical innovation: smart contracts. These are programmatically enforceable agreements that do not require a middleman to execute. With this, Ethereum allowed developers to create a multitude of decentralized applications, or dApps, on their platform. Among these were tokens, both fungible (like Bitcoin and Ethereum) and non-fungible, the latter of which are known as NFTs.

3.3. Emergence of NFTs

The real breakthrough for NFTs came in 2017 with a game, rather than a piece of art or a collectible. Known as CryptoKitties, it allowed players to purchase, collect, breed, and sell virtual cats. Each cat was unique and owned by the player, not the game developer, woven into the Ethereum blockchain through a standard called ERC-721, which was an interface for non-fungible tokens.

CryptoKitties marked the first mass-market use of NFTs and the beginning of their integration into digital economies. It demonstrated that digital uniqueness and scarcity could increase the value of digital assets dramatically.

3.4. NFTs Today

Since CryptoKitties, NFTs have expanded to encompass a vast variety of digital assets, from digital art and music to virtual real estate and digital collectibles. The fever around NFTs reached a climax in 2021 when a digital artwork by Beeple sold for $69 million at Christie's auction house.

Parallel to the excitement has been the rise of various platforms facilitating the creation, sale, and trade of NFTs. Some of the most popular ones include OpenSea, Rarible, and NBA Top Shot. These platforms make creating NFTs accessible to not just traditional artists, but also digital creators of all types.

Still, much like any nascent technology, NFTs have their share of controversies and challenges. Critics point out the environmental impact of maintaining the blockchain. The extreme volatility and speculative nature have raised questions about the sustainability of NFTs as a viable investment.

However, the potential in technology is huge. NFTs could revolutionize intellectual property rights, improve the transparency in art and music industries, democratize access to wealth generation, or even introduce new forms of social and economic interaction in the digital realm. In the hands of innovative thinkers and creators, there's no end to where NFTs might lead us.

The story of NFTs is far from over; in fact, it's barely just begun. As we continue to push the boundaries of what's possible in the digital world, NFTs will undoubtedly play a crucial role in defining how uniqueness and ownership are perceived in the digital age. So, whether we engage with them as creators, collectors, or investors, understanding their origins and evolution will be key to making sense of a world increasingly underpinned by digital assets and blockchain technology.

Despite the controversies and challenges, one cannot deny that NFTs represent a unique intersection of technology, art, culture, and economy, a new kind of asset class that has opened a Pandora's box of possibilities for an existence flanked by physical reality on one side and digital reality on the other. Regardless of one's technological prowess or knowledge, this new world demands our attention, as it continues to shape and influence our futuristic existence in unimaginable ways.

Chapter 4. Blockchain: The Foundation of NFTs

The inception of Non-Fungible Tokens (NFTs) in the digital world is deeply rooted in a revolutionary technology known as blockchain. To fully grasp the potential and mechanics of NFTs, it is essential to understand the bedrock upon which they are built: the blockchain.

Before embarking on a detailed foray into blockchain, we should first define it. In layman's terms, a blockchain is a type of database. However, instead of being housed in a single location, the data in a blockchain is distributed across a network of computers, or 'nodes'. This decentralized storage mechanism is one of the features that makes blockchain so unique and versatile.

4.1. Decentralization and Its Benefits

In a traditional centralized system, whether it be a banking institution or a digital art platform, all information is stored in one location. In contrast, in a decentralized system supported by blockchain technology, there is no single point of failure. Because data is distributed across a network of computers, it is extremely difficult to tamper or interfere with, as changes or fraudulent activities become immediately noticeable and can be cross-referenced with other copies of the ledger. This creates a transparent, secure, and reliable system, making blockchain a solid and trustworthy foundation for NFTs.

4.2. Understanding Blockchain Transactions

When we use cryptocurrencies, such as Bitcoin, or trade NFTs, a record of the transaction is created. This transaction record includes crucial details like the sender, the receiver, the date, and the amount of the cryptocurrency, or the unique data of the NFT art or item. The transaction needs verification from multiple nodes in the network before being approved.

Once the transaction is verified, it is then clustered with other verified transactions into a 'block'. This block is then added to the 'chain' of previous blocks, resulting in a blockchain.

4.3. The Immutable Nature of the Blockchain

One key aspect of blockchain technology is its immutability, meaning that once a transaction has been verified and added to a block, it cannot be tampered with or altered. This feature safeguards NFTs against forgery and duplication. Besides offering guaranteed digital ownership, this also ensures the provenance and authenticity of an NFT, since each token can be traced back to its original creation.

4.4. Utility of Smart Contracts in the Blockchain

At the center of NFT transactions are 'smart contracts', self-executing contracts with the terms of the agreement directly written into code. Built on the Ethereum blockchain, these smart contracts allow for secure, transparent, and tamper-proof transactions of NFTs.

More than just a record of transaction, a smart contract can also be programmed to perform specific tasks when events follow a predefined sequence. For instance, it can be used to split and distribute royalty payments among multiple parties every time an NFT is sold.

4.5. The Role of Blockchain in NFT Provenance

NFTs' exclusive nature is guaranteed by the blockchain. When an NFT is minted, its unique data is recorded on the blockchain. Each time an NFT is bought, sold, or transferred, a new record is created, preserving the entire history of that NFT. This full traceability grants full transparency in verifying NFT ownership and authenticity.

4.6. Challenges and Opportunities

Despite the innovative solutions provided by blockchain, it also brings its share of challenges. Energy consumption, scalability, and accessibility are among the major concerns revolving around the technology. However, even with these challenges, the potential of blockchain as the underpinning of NFTs and other decentralized applications far outweighs its hitches.

With advancements toward scalable solutions like Layer 2 protocols, and more energy-efficient consensus mechanisms like Proof-of-Stake, blockchain continues to evolve. It's paving the way for new digital landscapes where art, collectibles, real estate, and more, exist in new, fungible, and dynamic forms.

In summary, blockchain is the lifeblood that gives NFTs their unique characteristics. Its decentralized nature, coupled with the security and transparency it provides, make it an ideal infrastructure for the development and distribution of NFTs. As we continue to navigate this digital era, understanding blockchain becomes key in unlocking and unleashing the potential of NFTs.

Chapter 5. Demystifying Cryptography and Smart Contracts

The intriguing facet of the digital realm draws its roots from a critical discipline: cryptography. As the bedrock of NFTs and most other digital assets, cryptography involves complex algorithms that secure the information you're sending over the internet.

Encryption, an essential component of cryptography, converts plaintext into an unintelligible format, or cipher-text, while decryption reverses the process, changing cipher-text back to plaintext. This perplexing transformation shields information from interference by unauthorized third parties.

Two prime types of encryption exist: symmetric and asymmetric cryptography. Symmetric cryptography, the elder of the two, employs the same key for both encryption and decryption. The primary challenge here is secure distribution of the secret key to the concerned parties.

On the contrary, asymmetric cryptography uses two distinct keys, the public key, known to everyone, and a private key, held secret by its owner. What is encrypted with the public key can only be decrypted by the respective private key. This method, known as Public Key Infrastructure (PKI), forms the basis for secure digital communicative practices.

5.1. Strong Roots Demand Secure Foundations

Now that we've explained the workings of cryptography, let's delve into how this integrates with Non-Fungible Tokens. The answer lies in the wonders of blockchain technology, a series of interlinked blocks of data managed by a vast network of computers. Each block records a bundle of transactions and is secured by cryptographic techniques, ensuring data integrity and preventing tampering.

This incorporation of cryptography into blockchain technology enables the creation of 'digital trust.' Users, despite being dispersed across the globe and devoid of interaction apart from the digital sphere, can place trust in the functioning of the system due to its secure and decentralized nature. This trust factor makes digital transactions, including NFTs, possible.

5.2. From Scripts to Smart Contracts

Blockchains, such as Ethereum - a popular choice for creating NFTs - run on computer programs known as smart contracts. In essence, these are scripts or algorithms that self-execute once certain pre-determined conditions are met. They automate and enforce the terms of an agreement digitally, eliminating the need for intermediaries.

Smart contracts offer security, predictability, and transparency - qualities desirable in any undertaking, especially in the digital domain, marked by mistrust and obfuscation. As an example, the sale and purchase of an NFT can be set up within a smart contract that transfers the digital asset from the seller to the buyer only when the agreed money changes hands.

5.3. Behind the Scenes of a Smart Contract

A common type of smart contract on the Ethereum platform utilizes the Ethereum Virtual Machine (EVM). This smart contract is written in a programming language called Solidity. This contract once deployed is immutable - it can neither be edited nor deleted. This feature, although advantageous for security purposes, necessitates correct coding; mistakes can prove costly.

An Ethereum smart contract consists of multiple components, such as:

1. State variables: These represent the 'state' or condition of the smart contract.

2. Functions: Functions define the rules which govern changes in the state.

3. Events: These enable the smart contract's utilization of the Ethereum blockchain's logging facilities.

4. Modifiers: Modifiers are useful in condition checking before function execution.

5.4. The Intricate Dance of Non-Fungible Tokens and Smart Contracts

While fungible tokens like Bitcoin or Ether are interchangeable, Non-Fungible Tokens showcase uniqueness. Each token has a distinct identifier, carrying individual traits, hence not exchangeable on a like-for-like basis.

NFTs leverage the Ethereum platform's ERC-721 standard for their creation and transaction. This standard defines the minimum functions that a smart contract must implement to manage, transfer, and provide information about each unique token.

NFT smart contracts thus include ownership details and token metadata, which speak to the NFT's uniqueness. They have a mapping of token IDs to addresses, which define who owns a given token, ensuring clear property rights. There's also a permission mapping which decides who can transfer a given token, thereby solidifying the control of ownership.

In conclusion, the world of NFTs can seem complex and convoluted, with the intermingling of cryptography, blockchain technology, and smart contracts. We hope this chapter has made these subjects more approachable and understandable. By illuminating the underlying mechanism, we've taken the first step in unraveling the intricacies of Non-Fungible Tokens. As we move forward in this foray into digital innovation, let's open our minds and hearts to the infinite possibilities that this digital renaissance presents.

Chapter 6. NFTs in the Art Scene: Revolution or Novelty?

In 2021, the sale of an artwork called "Everydays: The First 5000 Days" for over $69 million left the art world reeling. This digital artwork, by the artist Beeple, was sold as a non-fungible token. The art industry suddenly found itself grappling with a new medium of artistic expression and commerce. This episode serves as a perfect starting point to unravel the threads tying NFTs to the art scene.

A non-fungible token, or NFT, is a type of digital asset that uses blockchain technology to authenticate and verify its ownership. Each NFT carries with it a unique digital signature, making it impossible to duplicate or forge. This has important implications for the art world, where fraud, forgery, and unclear provenance of artworks have been longstanding issues.

6.1. NFTs: Revolutionizing Artistic Ownership and Authenticity

Traditionally, the value of an artwork hinges on its authenticity and originality. The digital realm, being infinitely replicable, posed a challenge to this notion. Digital art has typically been seen as less valuable, largely because it can be copied and distributed infinitely, diluting the 'scarcity' that often drives the value of physical artworks.

NFTs change this equation. With unique metadata and identifiers embedded into each token, digital artworks gain the possibility of singular ownership. Because they are built on the Ethereum Blockchain, NFTs generate a tamper-proof history of ownership, a decentralized certificate of authenticity where the validity of the artwork and the ownership history can be trusted.

6.2. Virtual Galleries and Marketplaces

While initial interest in NFTs was primarily from the crypto community, they have found a coming-of-age within the artistic community. Digital artists can now mint, display, and sell their art as NFTs through various online marketplaces like OpenSea, Rarible, and Foundation. Notably, digital art platforms like SuperRare and Nifty Gateway have engaged renowned artists and enthusiasts in curating and purchasing these unique assets, enabling new dynamics of engagement.

Beyond this, virtual reality galleries add a spatial dimension to the viewing of digital art. Spatial platforms like Cryptovoxels and Decentraland allow anyone to host and attend exhibitions, opening up new ways for artists and collectors to interact and trade.

6.3. The Democratization of Art

Historically, the art world has been dependent on gatekeepers – curators, galleries, art critics – who acted as the arbiters of value. NFTs have the potential to democratize the art world. An artist can bypass traditional gatekeepers, list their work directly on a marketplace, and find their audience.

Moreover, NFTs allow artists to embed royalties into their work, meaning they can earn a percentage of sales every time their artwork changes hands. This is a massive shift in the economics of art and provides a more sustainable income model for artists in the long run.

6.4. It's Not All Rosy: Critiques and Controversies

Critics of NFTs in the art world levy several charges. The sustainability of NFTs is questioned given their environmental impact, as the energy consumption associated with creating, buying, and selling NFTs on the Ethereum blockchain is sizable.

Further, as with any democratized platform, the proliferation of low-quality content is a concern. The lack of regulation or curation may lead to a 'dilution' of artistic quality. There's also the fear of opportunistic exploitation of the hype around NFTs, with a risk of promoting a 'gold rush' mentality rather than a genuine appreciation of digital art.

6.5. The Future: A Balancing Act

NFTs have undoubtedly sandwiched themselves into art discourse. They've opened up an array of new possibilities for creators, collectors, and platforms, making digital art an asset class of its own. But they've also garnered criticism and sparked important conversations about sustainability and the dynamics of a liberalized art world.

It remains to be seen whether NFTs represent a revolution or a novelty. To effectively contribute toward a sustained evolution of the art scene, there's a need to address the environmental impact and to promote education around the consumption and trading of NFTs. Moreover, with more formalized involvement from established institutions, we could see a version of NFT-based art commerce that balances the benefits of democratization with the need for some level of oversight.

Whether it's a revolution or not, one thing's certain: NFTs have made a mark on the art scene, and the ripples of their impact are set to evolve for years to come.

Chapter 7. Digital Collectibles: The Advent of Virtual Ownership

It all started with an innocent curiosity, a desire to play, and inherent human fascination for collecting and owning unique items. Digital collectibles have birthed an intriguing and innovative form of virtual ownership.

Before navigating further down this rabbit hole, it's essential to understand what digital collectibles are. These are unique or limited-edition virtual items, each possessing its own identity, history, and value – from digital art and music to virtual pets and real estate in simulated environments.

7.1. The Genesis of Digital Collectibles

Perhaps the first digital collectible that achieved mainstream recognition was CryptoKitties. Launched in 2017 by a Vancouver-based start-up called Dapper Labs, CryptoKitties transcended the definition of a game. Players could purchase, breed, and even sell digital cats, each with a unique genetic code and appearance. More than just pixelated pets, each CryptoKitty represented a unique non-fungible token on the Ethereum blockchain, hence becoming intrinsically valuable.

This disruptive concept shaped a new reality where owning virtual assets wasn't just plausible, but also potentially profitable. It paved the path to a myriad of virtual universes, each with their exclusive collection of digital assets.

7.2. The Intersection of Tech and Fandom

The technological boom coincides with the rise of fandom culture. Today, you can find major sports leagues issuing digital collectibles and fans eager to secure a digital piece of their favorite sports moments. NBA Top Shot releases limited-edition "moments" which are essentially digital sports cards, allowing fans to own these high-definition video clips. These moments, backed by blockchain, hold real value, and can be sold or traded within the community.

In the music world, artists are tapping into NFTs as a new distribution and consumption model. Take Kings of Leon, for instance, they released their latest album as an NFT, meshing art, music, and virtual merchandise into a single digital collectible.

These instances illustrate a remarkable shift in the culture of fandom, where emotional value intertwines with monetary worth, fueled further by technology.

7.3. Placing Value on the Virtual

Assigning value to something intangible might appear paradoxical on the surface, especially when we're conditioned to perceive value in terms of physicality - its size, weight, or material. However, virtual assets carry a new kind of value: a blend of financial, sentimental, and social worth.

The financial value of these digital collectibles arises from the elemental laws of economics – supply and demand. If a digital asset is unique or limited-edition, its scarcity generates demand, driving up its price.

Sentimental value often comes from a personal connection or bond with the virtual object, like a rare card of a favorite sports personality, a digital pet, or a piece of art from an admired artist.

Finally, social value is derived from the prestige or bragging rights associated with owning a high-priced or coveted digital asset. Think of it as a virtual status symbol.

7.4. Virtual Reality, Virtual Opportunities

As we push the boundaries further, while remaining grounded on blockchain technology, we encounter virtual real estate - a curious intersection of the real and virtual world.

Platforms like Decentraland and Cryptovoxels enable users to purchase, develop, and monetize digital plots of land. This could range from simple virtual art galleries to full-fledged digital casinos running on microtransactions.

Though on the outskirts of the mainstream, virtual real estate has started turning heads. Sandbox, another virtual world, recently sold digital land worth $3 million in just a few hours.

7.5. The Dark Side of Virtual Ownership

There's no denying the allure of digital collectibles, with their promise of rarity, uniqueness, and decentralization. Yet, it's essential to tread with caution.

The lack of regulation in this digital frontier can be a double-edged sword. Scams, hacks, and counterfeits are real risks. Plus, given the volatility and speculation around digital assets, it's not uncommon to witness wild price swings.

Then, there's the environmental impact. Blockchains are notoriously energy-hungry, given the computationally intensive operations they perform. For instance, Ethereum, the leading platform for NFTs, uses a "proof-of-work" consensus algorithm which has come under scrutiny for its high energy usage.

7.6. A Glimpse into the Future

Currently, we're merely at the advent of virtual ownership. Going forward, the boundaries of digital collectibles will continue expanding, powered by developments in technology. We might see virtual assets playing a significant role in metaverses - where virtual and augmented realities converge.

Given this, the concept of ownership is due for an upheaval, one where your most valuable possession might exist solely as an entry on a digital ledger. And while the images might be virtual, the implications are most certainly real.

However, the most exciting part is that this evolution is happening in real-time, and we have front-row seats to witness it - a journey as mesmerizing as the wonder-filled rabbit hole we've just delved into. The advent of digital collectibles and the dawn of virtual ownership, indeed, is only just beginning.

Chapter 8. Technical Pitfalls and Challenges in the NFT Space

Non-Fungible Tokens (NFTs) are an innovative and disruptive technology, challenging the status quo of several industries. As promising as the technology may be, it's not without significant technical pitfalls and challenges. It's crucial to understand these potential trip-ups and hurdles in order to better grasp the intricacies of the NFT spectrum and contribute effectively to its growth.

8.1. Scalability Issues

One of the major challenges faced by blockchain technologies, including Ethereum, the most commonly used blockchain for creating and trading NFTs, is the issue of scalability. Currently, the Ethereum network can process around 15 transactions per second. In comparison, traditional systems like credit cards can manage tens of thousands during the same timeframe.

The limitation in transaction throughput leads to slower confirmation times, especially when the network is congested. It also results in higher gas costs as users are forced to outbid each other to get their transactions processed faster. This significantly affects the feasibility of creating and trading NFTs. Given that these digital assets often hold high monetary value, ensuring swift and affordable transactions is a fundamental requirement of any NFT platform.

Some solutions to this issue are the implementation of sharding and Layer 2 scaling solutions like rollups and Plasma. Sharding involves partitioning the Ethereum network into smaller parts or shards, each capable of processing transactions and smart contracts. Layer 2 solutions, on the other hand, process transactions off the main blockchain, offering faster and cheaper transactions.

8.2. Environmental Concerns

Another challenge with NFTs stems from the concern over their environmental impact. This problem arises primarily due to the energy-intensive proof-of-work algorithm utilized by blockchains like Ethereum. The process of verifying transactions and adding them to the blockchain, known as mining, requires significant computational power and hence, energy.

The rise of NFTs and the consequential increase in transactions on the Ethereum network have led to a surge in energy consumption. NFTs have, as a result, faced criticism for their environmental footprint. While Ethereum plans to mitigate these issues by moving to a more energy-efficient consensus mechanism called proof-of-stake, until this transition is complete, the environmental concerns remain a real challenge.

8.3. Interoperability and Standardization

Interoperability, the ability for different systems and networks to understand and interact with each other, is another technical issue in the NFT space. Currently, the NFT landscape is quite fragmented, with different blockchains and marketplaces all establishing their own way of creating, storing, and trading NFTs.

Without a standard set of rules, it would be difficult for different NFT platforms to communicate and interoperate. This lack of interoperability makes it challenging for users to manage and exchange NFTs across different networks, limiting the usability and accessibility of NFTs.

Efforts like the ERC721 and ERC1155 standards, representing the earliest steps towards interoperability and standardization of NFTs on the Ethereum blockchain, are a step in the right direction. These protocols establish a standard set of rules for creating NFTs, making them less complex and more interoperable.

8.4. Legality and Copyright

There's also the issue of legality and copyright given the digital nature of NFTs. Since NFTs often represent artwork or other forms of creative content, the ownership rights of these assets can be a point of contention. Copying and tokenizing art without permission, or even creating fake NFTs, have become significant concerns.

While the blockchain records every transaction and thereby provides a level of proof of ownership, it doesn't prevent copyright violations if stolen content is minted as an NFT. Improving the copyright protection on these digital assets will be a major hurdle to overcome.

As these technical challenges show, the NFT space, though promising, is still in its early stages and dealing with some major issues. Addressing these will require a focus on continued development of infrastructure, standards, and regulations. As we move towards resolving these issues, the NFT space will continue to represent an exciting and dynamic field in the digital world.

Chapter 9. Legalities and Intellectual Property in the World of NFTs

The emergence of Non-Fungible Tokens (NFTs) has opened an entirely new debate about the legalities and intellectual property rights on the digital platform. As much as NFTs promise opportunities, they also present a maze of legal challenges that need to be understood and traversed.

9.1. The Intellectual Property Landscape of NFTs

To begin, it should be clarified that an NFT doesn't grant the buyer ownership of the digital asset itself but the 'token' that proves its uniqueness and their ownership of that token. It's akin to having a signed painting - the signature is unique, but doesn't provide ownership rights to the artist's work. In this light, NFTs are not significantly different from traditional art sales, emphasizing the need for a robust intellectual property system around these tokens.

Understanding how copyrights work is therefore pivotal in NFT transactions. When a digital artist creates work, they automatically own the copyright to that work. When they mint an NFT to represent the work, they are not transferring the actual copyright to the buyer but rather giving them 'display rights'. These rights can vary from case to case and need to be explicitly stated.

9.2. Legal Positions on NFTs

Presently, the legislation around NFTs is largely undefined. However, several legal positions can be inferred based on existing laws. Different jurisdictions will have varying laws that might or might not cover elements of NFTs. This lack of unified legalities could cause friction between jurisdictions, particularly those with more rigid frameworks.

NFTs also tiptoe into the territory of contract law. Any terms and conditions set by the platform and agreed upon by the buyer during the purchase act as a contract. However, these contracts can be murky, given that they could potentially cover a mix of physical and digital rights.

9.3. Challenges in Applying Existing Laws to NFTs

Applying traditional intellectual property laws to NFTs presents several challenges - mainly that these laws were not designed to tackle the complexities of the digital world. Copyright infringement, for instance, becomes more problematic in the borderless digital sphere as opposed to the well-defined physical world.

Moreover, most existing litigation around copyright infringement requires proof of a certain threshold of loss, which isn't easy to demonstrate in the world of NFTs. Also, the decentralization aspect of blockchain means there's no central authority that can be held responsible or officiate over claims.

9.4. The Case for Bespoke NFT Legislation

The unique features of NFTs, their embedded contracts, and variable rights point to the need for new, specific legislation. Just as data privacy laws are being reformed following the intensification of digital operations, NFT legislation needs a similar renovation.

Such legislation could clarify essential matters such as the precise legal status of an NFT, the terms of contractual obligations, the rights and limits of an NFT owner, and the consequences of copyright violations.

9.5. NFTs and the Future of Intellectual Property

The realm of NFTs has broad implications for the future of intellectual property. Creative works that had been deemed hard to monetize, like tweets or digital images, can now be assigned value, opening up new avenues for artists to profit from their work.

Moreover, NFTs offer a strong tool for combating digital forgery and preserving authenticity. By combining traditional intellectual property laws with the verifiability and immutability of blockchain, a stronger, more efficient model for protecting and enforcing intellectual property could materialize.

However, the future also brings scenarios where NFTs could potentially compromise intellectual property, such as in the case of 'minting' someone else's work without permission, giving rise to instances of 'crypto theft'.

In conclusion, navigating around the legalities and intellectual property in the world of NFTs is an uncharted territory fraught with challenges. As we move forward, the intertwining, and often conflicting, interests of all parties — creators, buyers, platforms, and jurisdictions — will need to come to the forefront. There will need to be a balance struck between fostering creativity, protecting rights, and ensuring regulation in a digitized, decentralized world. It is a complicated jigsaw, but one which states, law firms, platforms and artists will have to solve together.

Chapter 10. Investing in NFTs: Risks and Rewards

Investing in the vibrant world of Non-Fungible Tokens (NFTs) can be exhilarating, filled with both potential windfalls and significant risks. From art enthusiasts to celebrities and even to the average investor dipping their toes into the crypto world, NFTs present a new avenue for speculation, collection, and investment.

10.1. Defining the Investment in NFTs

Investing in NFTs, at its core, is the act of paying cryptocurrency for digital assets stored and authenticated on the blockchain. Blockchain technology ensures that these digital assets are unique and verifiable, leading to their non-fungible nature - no two NFTs are exactly alike. This starkly contrasts with fungible cryptocurrencies like Bitcoin, where each individual coin holds the exact same value as another.

You can compare this investment to acquiring physical collectibles such as rare baseball cards or pieces of art. However, the significant difference lies in the digital format, which allows for the democratization of ownership, the possibility of fractional ownership, and potentially vast access to a global market, among other benefits. The downside includes market volatility, lack of regulation, and issues with intellectual property rights.

10.2. Identifying Potential Rewards

Investing in NFTs can yield noteworthy rewards. The most obvious is the potential for high returns. For instance, an NFT artwork by digital artist Beeple, sold by Christie's for almost $70 million, highlights the extraordinary "gold rush" potential that has grabbed the attention of investors worldwide.

However, it's important to stress that such cases are not the norm, and investing in NFTs should be driven by more than merely the hope of massive returns.

NFTs can also serve as a form of portfolio diversification, especially for those already invested in cryptocurrencies. With this new asset class, investors can expand and diversify their holdings, spreading risk across different types of investments.

Another reward comes in the form of connection and access to exclusive communities. This is particularly the case with NFTs that serve as 'keys' to virtual clubs or experiences, providing owners with exclusive membership rights.

10.3. Pinpointing Potential Risks

Despite the excitement around NFTs, it's essential to scrutinize the associated risks, the first of which is volatility. NFT prices are notoriously volatile due to a combination of factors: hype, investor sentiment, evolving technologies, and regulatory discussions. Investing in NFTs without understanding this potential for significant price swings can lead to substantial losses.

Lack of regulation is another significant risk. With the novelty of NFTs and the absence of a regulatory framework, investors are in largely unchartered territory. This can lead to manipulation and fraud, as nefarious agents can exploit the system's lack of transparency.

Furthermore, issues around intellectual property (IP) rights are critical. While purchasing an NFT might provide ownership of a unique digital asset, it doesn't necessarily grant IP rights. This distinction means that while you might own a unique copy of an artist's work, the artist can still retain rights to reproduce or sell similar copies.

Finally, there's a risk in the potential lack of liquidity. While the NFTs market has grown in volume and popularity, the demand for individual NFTs may not always exist.

10.4. Taking the Informed Leap

Navigating the NFT investment arena necessitates due diligence, risk management strategies, and a healthy dose of caution. As with any investment, knowledge is power. Conduct extensive research, keep abreast of market trends, use secure wallets for transactions, and perhaps most importantly, always be prepared for volatility.

In terms of risk management, it's essential not to invest more than you're willing to lose. Diversify your investments, balance high-risk investments with more stable counterparts, and consider seeking advice from financial advisors or individuals with solid experience in the NFT market.

10.5. The Future of NFT Investing

The future of NFTs is still unwritten. Trends suggest that we're likely to see further integration of NFTs into digital experiences, whether in virtual reality, video games, decentralized finance (DeFi) platforms, or digital art. There's significant potential for market growth and technological innovation.

However, a closer look also indicates a need for consolidation, market maturity, and improved regulatory oversight. Market wisdom will need to evolve for long-term stability, profitability, and resistance to manipulation.

In essence, while the world of NFTs is teeming with potential rewards, the risks are equally prominent, a reflection of this rousing but unpredictable market. By understanding the inherent challenges and approaching with a sound strategy, you can invest in NFTs with your eyes wide open.

Chapter 11. The Future of NFTs: Predictions and Potential Implications

As we contemplate our journey into the future of Non-Fungible Tokens (NFTs), it is essential to understand that this road is still being built. However, based on current trends and advancements, a few well-informed predictions can be drawn about the possibilities that the future holds.

11.1. The Immersion of Virtual and Physical Worlds

In the future, we may see a nexus between the physical and digital worlds, with NFTs playing a crucial role in this unification. Digital ownership can extend to real-world assets, and vice-versa. We could see homes, cars, and other valuable items tokenized into NFTs while digital assets may also become physical, such as an NFT of a digital artwork becoming a real-world painting.

Companies may make use of AR (Augmented Reality) and VR (Virtual Reality) technology to provide a more immersive experience for NFT owners. Imagine walking around in a virtual gallery, surrounded by your collection of NFT artwork, or attending a virtual music concert of your favorite artist, the ticket for which is an NFT in your digitized wallet.

11.2. Democratizing the Art and Music Industries

One fascinating aspect of NFTs is their potential to democratize the art and music industries. With NFTs, artists can sell their work directly to consumers, avoiding the need for intermediaries such as galleries and music labels. In turn, this practice can lead to more egalitarian revenue distribution, allowing artists to take the lion's share of earnings from their creative output.

In the future, this could even shift the power dynamics within creative sectors, offering voices to those hitherto unheard. Creative works of previously underrepresented groups may gain newfound visibility and acceptance in a world where ownership and distribution are more equitable.

11.3. The Influence of Big Tech

Tech giants such as Facebook, Google, and Amazon could also integrate NFTs into their ecosystems. Much as social media titans now provide a platform for user-created content, they may soon serve as a marketplace for digital goods underpinned by NFTs.

Meanwhile, the unity of big tech and NFTs may face considerable pushback. Regulation, antitrust issues, and public sentiment could all act as potential speed bumps on this road. How these corporations manage this integration will be a vital aspect of NFT's future.

11.4. Environmental Considerations

The environmental impact of NFTs, built on energy-intensive blockchains like Ethereum, is a significant concern that requires an urgent response if this promising technology is to be sustainable in the future. Developers and blockchain architects are already researching and implementing more sustainable methods such as proof-of-stake (PoS) consensus mechanism to counter the blockchain's carbon footprint.

The future may see environment-friendly blockchains becoming the norm, a departure from the current field dominated by power-hungry models like Ethereum's current proof-of-work setup.

11.5. The Evolution of Copyright Law

As NFTs include various rights to digital objects, they challenge the traditional notions of intellectual property. The current ruling on these digital assets is somewhat murky, and we may see a shift in copyright law to accommodate the changes brought about by NFTs.

In each country, policymakers, legislators, and legal scholars will need to define the legal boundaries in the world of NFTs. Their decisions can have profound consequences for the growth and spread of this technology.

11.6. The Potential Pitfalls

While NFTs offer a plethora of possibilities, their road to becoming a mainstay of the digital world is not devoid of challenges. Scams, frauds, and concerns regarding money laundering have already made headlines, and solutions must be found to safeguard buyers and sellers.

Additionally, the volatility of the cryptocurrency market, which directly impacts the value of NFTs, is an unavoidable problem. Measures to stabilize this erratic aspect of NFTs could be instrumental in their wider adoption.

In conclusion, the future of NFTs appears both exciting and unpredictable. But one thing we can say with certainty is that NFTs will continually reshape our perception of art, ownership, and digital identity. As pioneers navigating this frontier, the challenges will be significant, but so too are the opportunities. In understanding and embracing the change NFTs bring about, we find ourselves equipped to script the narrative of the digital future.

39

www.ingramcontent.com/pod-product-compliance
Lightning Source LLC
Chambersburg PA
CBHW071047260726
48661CB00007B/3182